Ladybird

W9-CEX-189

FLIGHT

CONTENTS

page

INTO THE AIR

Stories about human beings' attempts to fly can be found in the earliest myths and legends. But it wasn't until 1783 that people actually were able to take to the sky.

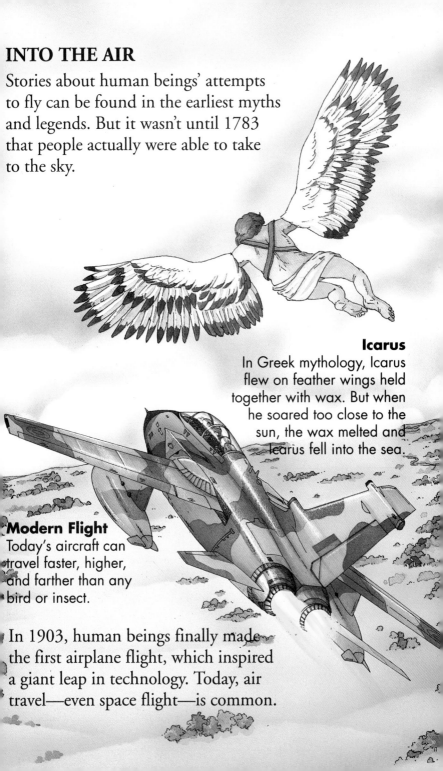

Icarus
In Greek mythology, Icarus flew on feather wings held together with wax. But when he soared too close to the sun, the wax melted and Icarus fell into the sea.

Modern Flight
Today's aircraft can travel faster, higher, and farther than any bird or insect.

In 1903, human beings finally made the first airplane flight, which inspired a giant leap in technology. Today, air travel—even space flight—is common.

HOT-AIR BALLOONS

In 1783, a sheep, a rooster, and a duck were the first living creatures to ride in a flying machine. They flew in a hot-air balloon. A few weeks later, Francois Pilatre de Rozier and Marquis d'Alrandres became the first people to fly in a hot-air balloon. They sailed across the city of Paris at an altitude of approximately 3,000 feet.

Ballooning
Created by the Montgolfier brothers of France, the first hot-air balloons were made of silk. Straw was burned to heat the air inside the balloon.

Hot air rises faster than cool air, so heating the air inside a balloon will make it rise. When the air inside is hot enough to overcome the weight of the balloon and its **payload**, the balloon rises. In modern hot-air balloons, the air is heated by propane, or gas, burners. The pilot brings the balloon down by opening a vent and letting out the hot air.

Height Control
Sand bags in the passenger compartment hold the balloon down before lift-off. Once in the air, the pilot makes the balloon rise by throwing out the sand bags.

Balloon Shapes
Modern hot-air balloons come in a wide variety of shapes, sizes, and colors.

AIRSHIPS

In the 1930s, the only way to cross the Atlantic Ocean by air was aboard an airship. Like hot-air balloons, airships rise because they are filled with something lighter than air. Instead of hot air, airships were filled with **hydrogen** gas. Larger airships were made of metal frames covered with cloth. Small engines, propellers, and rudders were used to steer them.

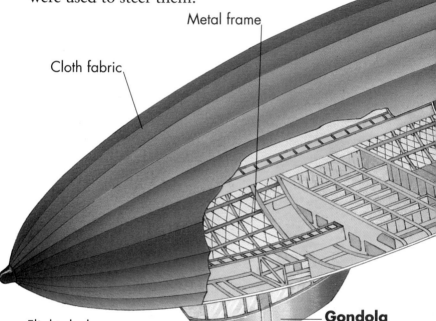

Metal frame

Cloth fabric

Flight deck

Gondola

Dangers of Airship Travel
In 1929, the *Graf Zeppelin* flew around the world. Airships, however, were slow and vulnerable to bad weather. By the end of the 1930s, after a series of disasters, airship travel came to an end.

Gondola
Passengers travelled in a **gondola** in the smaller airships.

Modern airships, called blimps, are smaller than those built in the 1930s and are filled with nonexplosive helium gas.

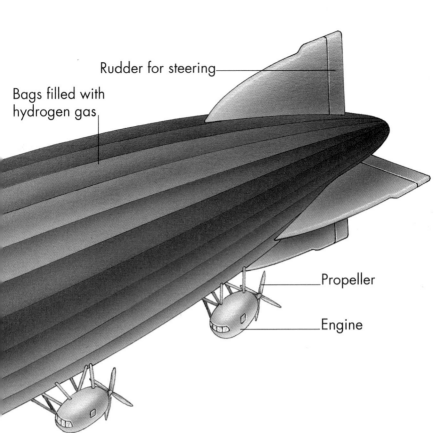

Rudder for steering

Bags filled with
hydrogen gas

Propeller

Engine

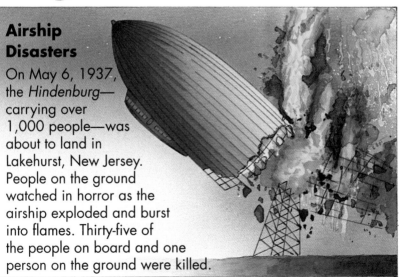

Airship Disasters

On May 6, 1937, the *Hindenburg*—carrying over 1,000 people—was about to land in Lakehurst, New Jersey. People on the ground watched in horror as the airship exploded and burst into flames. Thirty-five of the people on board and one person on the ground were killed.

THE SECRETS OF FLIGHT

There are four main forces acting on an airplane or bird as it flies—**lift, gravity, thrust,** and **drag.** To fly, an airplane or bird needs enough upward force, or lift, to overcome gravity. Thrust keeps a plane or bird moving forward through the air. Wind creates drag, which works against thrust to slow a bird or plane down. Drag is the same force you feel pushing against your face when you run.

Lift

Air rushes over the top of a wing faster than it travels underneath. This lifts a plane or bird into the air.

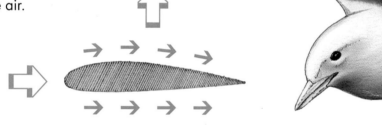

Airfoil

The top of a wing is curved and the bottom is flat. This shape is called an **airfoil** and is essential to winged flight. Because air flows faster over the top curved surface, the air pressure on this surface is lower. The greater air pressure under the bottom of the wing pushes the wing up, giving it lift.

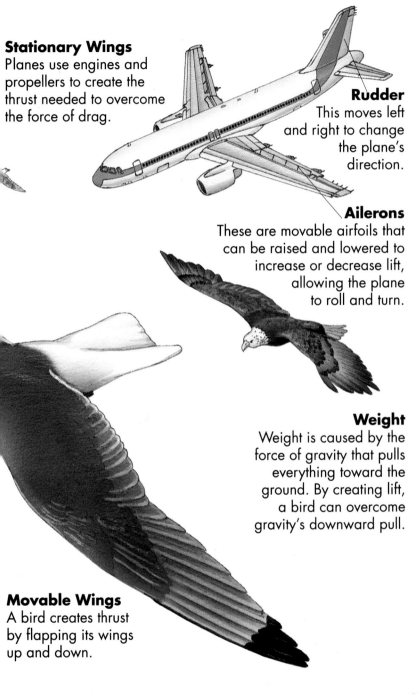

Stationary Wings
Planes use engines and propellers to create the thrust needed to overcome the force of drag.

Rudder
This moves left and right to change the plane's direction.

Ailerons
These are movable airfoils that can be raised and lowered to increase or decrease lift, allowing the plane to roll and turn.

Weight
Weight is caused by the force of gravity that pulls everything toward the ground. By creating lift, a bird can overcome gravity's downward pull.

Movable Wings
A bird creates thrust by flapping its wings up and down.

GLIDERS

A glider is a plane that flies without an engine. For takeoff a glider is towed by a plane or truck. After the glider rises in the air, the towing cable is released. Then rising updrafts of hot air, called **thermals**, lift the glider higher.

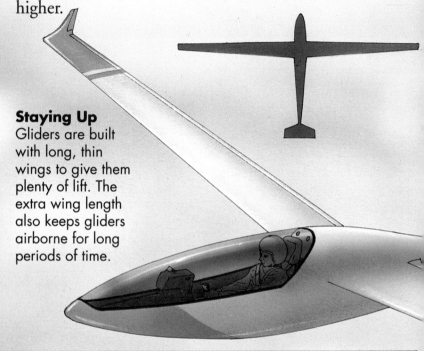

Staying Up
Gliders are built with long, thin wings to give them plenty of lift. The extra wing length also keeps gliders airborne for long periods of time.

Cayley's Glider
Sir George Cayley experimented with different glider shapes. His best design was a **triplane.** It had three sets of wings made from strong cloth stretched over a wooden frame. Cayley convinced his frightened coachman to make the first glider flight in 1853.

HANG GLIDING

Like birds, hang gliders fly on air currents. The wings of a hang glider are light, and the pilot hangs below them, secured in a harness and holding on to a steering bar. To take off, the pilot jumps from a steep hill or mountain.

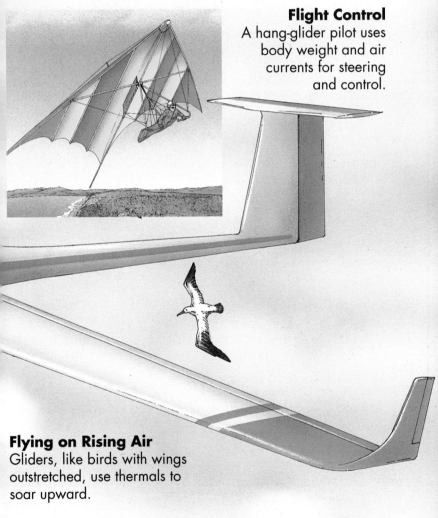

Flight Control
A hang-glider pilot uses body weight and air currents for steering and control.

Flying on Rising Air
Gliders, like birds with wings outstretched, use thermals to soar upward.

POWERED FLIGHT

In 1903, two American brothers, Orville and Wilbur Wright, first achieved sustained flight by a machine heavier than air. The Wright brothers were bicycle makers. They approached the problems of flight using models and wind tunnels. A steam engine was too heavy to power their flying machine, so they designed and built their own small, lightweight gasoline engine.

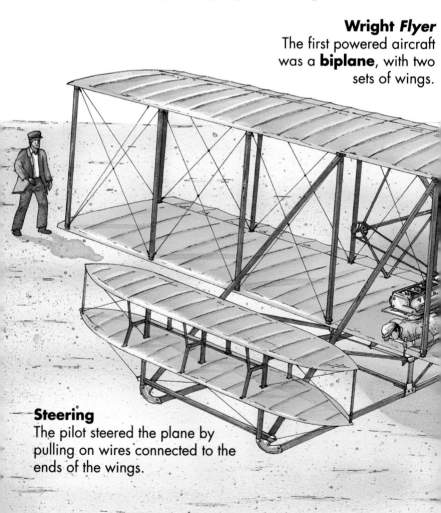

Wright *Flyer*
The first powered aircraft was a **biplane**, with two sets of wings.

Steering
The pilot steered the plane by pulling on wires connected to the ends of the wings.

The Wright brothers built *Flyer* in 1903 and tested it on a deserted beach near Kitty Hawk, North Carolina. Wilbur made the first attempt, but *Flyer* would not leave the ground. Three days later, on December 17, Orville took off and flew 120 feet. Although it only stayed in the air for twelve seconds, the Wright *Flyer* made the first powered flight in history.

MILESTONES OF EARLY FLIGHT

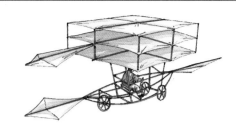

Pilot	Landmark	Date	Flight Report
Bartolomeu de Gusmão (Brazil)	Earliest recorded unmanned hot-air balloon flight	1709	The balloon was flown indoors
Henri Giffard (France)	Earliest flight in an airship	1852	The airship was powered by a steam engine
Wilbur Wright (United States)	First flight over 5 minutes	1904	*Flyer II* travelled over 2.5 miles
Paul Cornu (France)	The first flight in a helicopter	1907	Lifted less than two feet in the air
Louis Blériot (France)	First person to fly across the English Channel	1909	The flight took 36 minutes
Charles Lindbergh (United States)	First nonstop solo flight across the Atlantic	1927	The flight took 33 hours and 29 minutes
Amy Johnson (Britain)	First woman to fly solo from Britain to Australia	1930	The journey lasted 20 days
Amelia Earhart (United States)	First woman to fly solo over the Atlantic	1932	She flew from Newfoundland to Ireland
Wiley Post (United States)	First solo flight around the world	1933	The journey took 8 days

BOEING 747 JUMBO JET

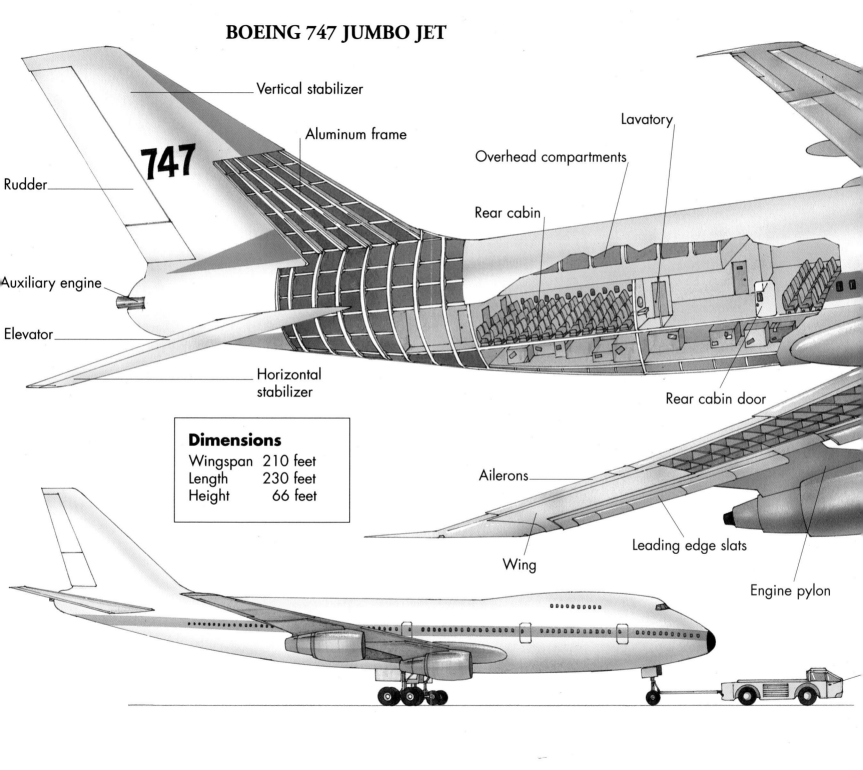

Vertical stabilizer

Lavatory

Overhead compartments

Aluminum frame

Rear cabin

747

Rudder

Auxiliary engine

Elevator

Horizontal stabilizer

Rear cabin door

Dimensions
Wingspan 210 feet
Length 230 feet
Height 66 feet

Ailerons

Wing

Leading edge slats

Engine pylon

THE AIRPORT

Outside the **terminal,** aircraft are serviced between flights. They are cleaned, refueled, and restocked with food and other supplies. When the passengers and luggage are on board, the aircraft prepares for takeoff.

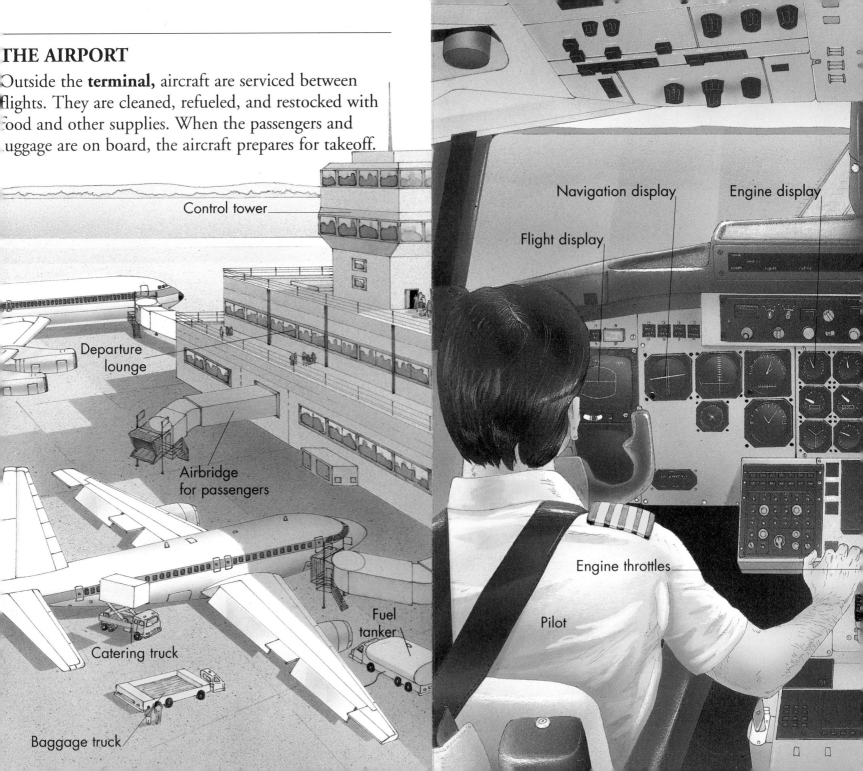

Control tower

Departure lounge

Airbridge for passengers

Catering truck

Baggage truck

Fuel tanker

Navigation display

Engine display

Flight display

Engine throttles

Pilot

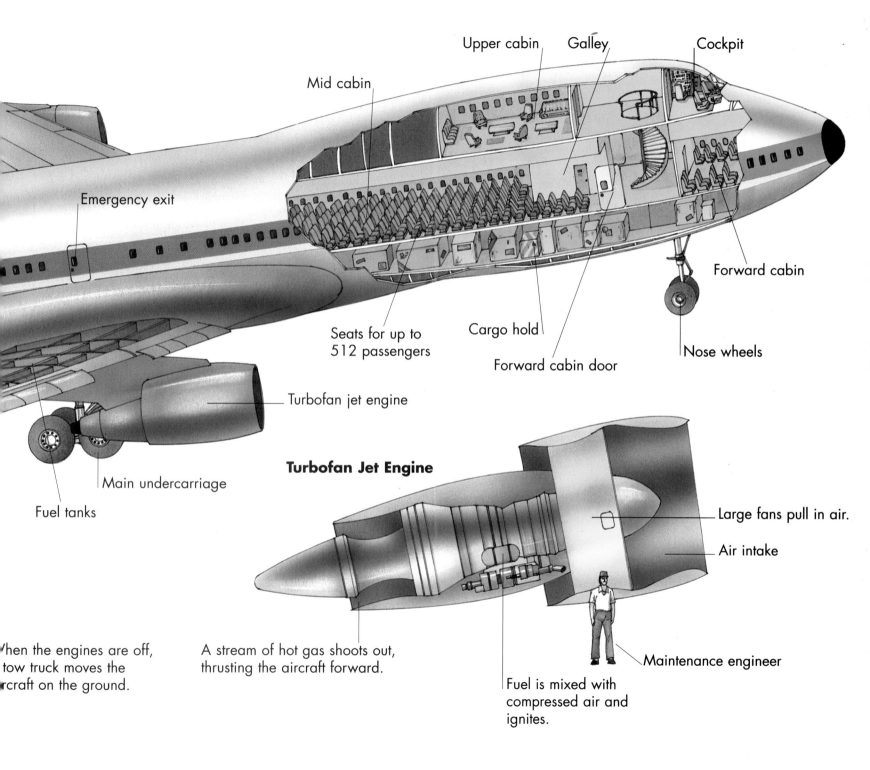

Upper cabin

Galley

Cockpit

Mid cabin

Emergency exit

Forward cabin

Seats for up to
512 passengers

Cargo hold

Forward cabin door

Nose wheels

Turbofan jet engine

Main undercarriage

Fuel tanks

Turbofan Jet Engine

Large fans pull in air.

Air intake

Maintenance engineer

hen the engines are off,
tow truck moves the
rcraft on the ground.

A stream of hot gas shoots out,
thrusting the aircraft forward.

Fuel is mixed with
compressed air and
ignites.

Overhead control panel

Control column

Brakes

Co-pilot

AIR TRAFFIC CONTROL

Using a complex system of electronic equipment, the air traffic control tower directs all planes on or near the runway of an airport. A plane may not land or **taxi** to the runway and take off until it has permission from the control tower.

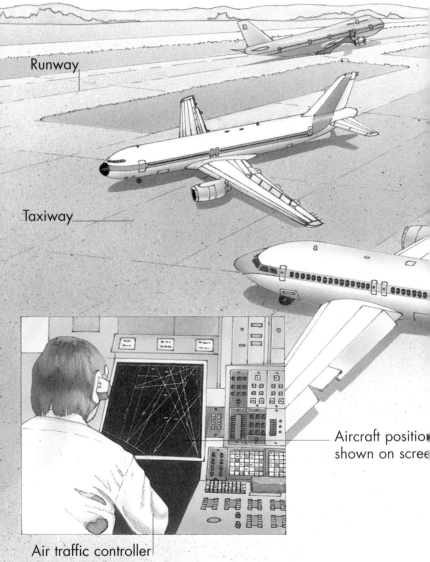

Runway

Taxiway

Aircraft position shown on scree

Air traffic controller

SEAPLANES

Seaplanes and flying boats take off and land on water. During the 1930s they carried passengers and mail. Today they are used mainly for transporation to and from remote areas. Seaplanes are also used for fighting large fires. The planes scoop up water as they fly over a sea or lake and then drop the water onto the fire.

Seaplane Floats
Some seaplanes have floats instead of wheels.

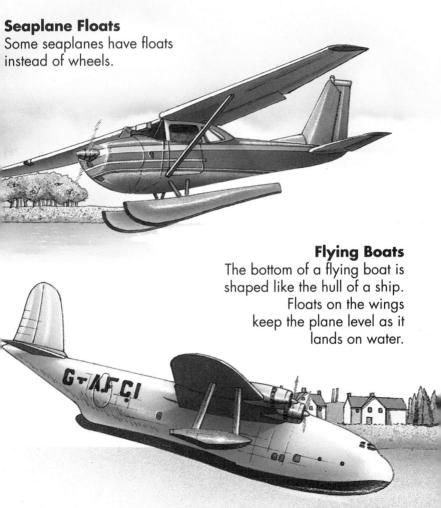

Flying Boats
The bottom of a flying boat is shaped like the hull of a ship. Floats on the wings keep the plane level as it lands on water.

JETS

In 1937, a new source of power—the jet engine—changed the world of flight. Jet engines enable modern planes to fly long distances at high speeds. A jet engine draws air in one end and mixes it with fuel. Then the compressed air and gases are forced out at great speed from the other end. This creates a powerful thrust that pushes the plane forward and upward.

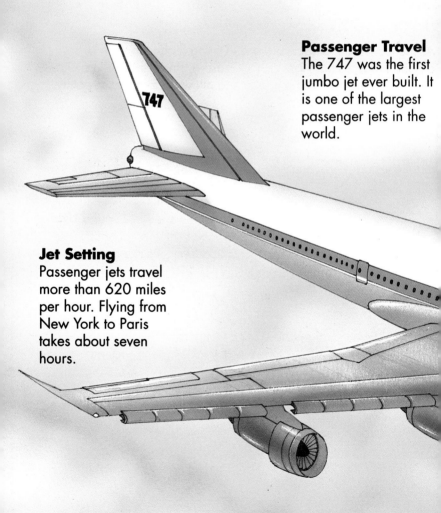

Passenger Travel
The 747 was the first jumbo jet ever built. It is one of the largest passenger jets in the world.

Jet Setting
Passenger jets travel more than 620 miles per hour. Flying from New York to Paris takes about seven hours.

THE *CONCORDE*

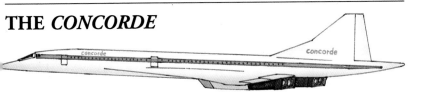

The *Concorde* carries 128 passengers and travels faster than the **speed of sound**. A flight from New York to Paris takes just over three hours.

As the *Concorde* takes off and lands, its nose is lowered so the pilot has a good view of the runway.

During flight, the nose is raised, streamlining the plane to allow air to travel smoothly around it.

Breaking the Sound Barrier
A jet's speed is measured in **Mach numbers**. Mach 1 equals the speed of sound. The *Concorde* cruises at Mach 2.2, or 2.2 times the speed of sound.

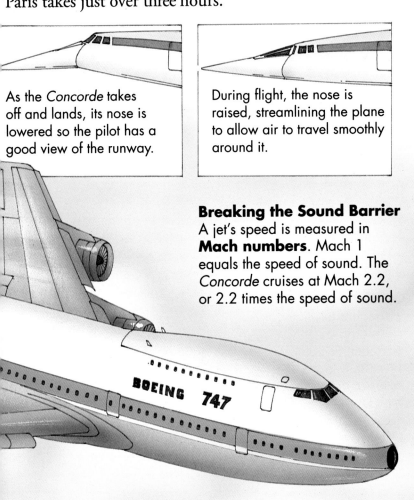

HELICOPTERS

Helicopters are different from airplanes in several ways. They land and take off vertically. Because they use landing pads instead of runways, they are used for special jobs, such as rescuing people from areas where planes cannot land, traffic reporting, fire fighting, and crop dusting.

Getting Around

The rotor blades allow the helicopter to maneuver up and down, forward and backward, and side-to-side. When they are kept level and spun quickly, the helicopter hovers.

Main Rotors

The main rotor blades are rotating airfoils that provide lift by spinning horizontally.

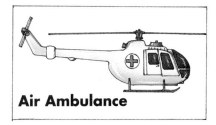

Air Ambulance

Military Helicopter

Tail Rotor

The tail rotor steers the helicopter left or right. It also keeps the helicopter from spinning out of control.

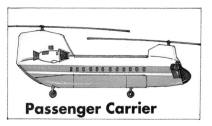

Passenger Carrier

An Early Helicopter

The first helicopter to fly successfully was built in 1907 by Paul Cornu. It stayed in the air for about a minute and flew less than two feet above the ground.

EARLY SPACE TRAVEL

Launching a rocket into space takes tremendous force. A huge amount of fuel is burned, producing gases that blast out of the bottom of the rocket with enough power to overcome Earth's gravity.

Several Engines
Each stage of a rocket has its own engines and fuel supply.

Fuel Consumption
As its fuel is used up, each stage is **jettisoned**.

Back to Earth
During the Apollo space program, the crew returned to Earth in the command module, and landed in the ocean.

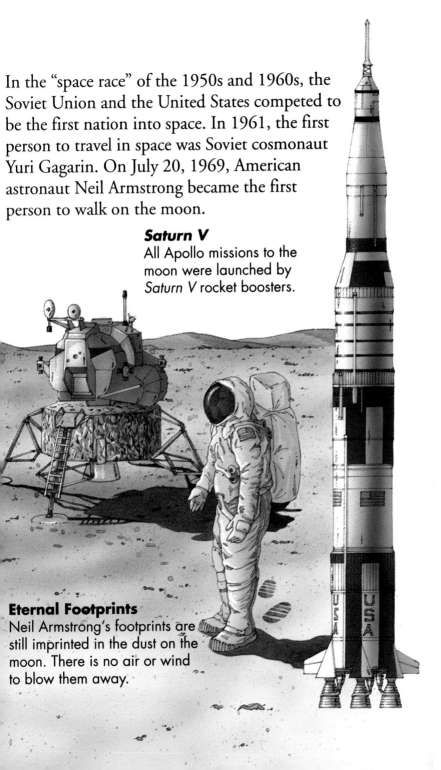

In the "space race" of the 1950s and 1960s, the Soviet Union and the United States competed to be the first nation into space. In 1961, the first person to travel in space was Soviet cosmonaut Yuri Gagarin. On July 20, 1969, American astronaut Neil Armstrong became the first person to walk on the moon.

Saturn V
All Apollo missions to the moon were launched by *Saturn V* rocket boosters.

Eternal Footprints
Neil Armstrong's footprints are still imprinted in the dust on the moon. There is no air or wind to blow them away.

SPACE SHUTTLES

Unlike earlier launch systems, which could only be used once, the space shuttle was designed to be flown several times. Flights, or missions, can last for weeks. The plane-like part of the shuttle is called the **orbiter**.

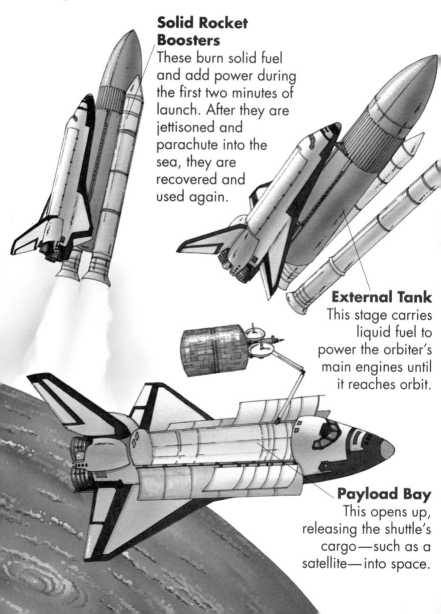

Solid Rocket Boosters
These burn solid fuel and add power during the first two minutes of launch. After they are jettisoned and parachute into the sea, they are recovered and used again.

External Tank
This stage carries liquid fuel to power the orbiter's main engines until it reaches orbit.

Payload Bay
This opens up, releasing the shuttle's cargo—such as a satellite—into space.

The space shuttles can carry satellites or telescopes into space in its payload bay. Astronauts often conduct experiments in on-board laboratories. They can also venture outside the shuttle in specially designed spacesuits.

Space Walks

Outside the shuttle, astronauts wear powered backpacks that propel them through space.

Hand controls

Thrusters

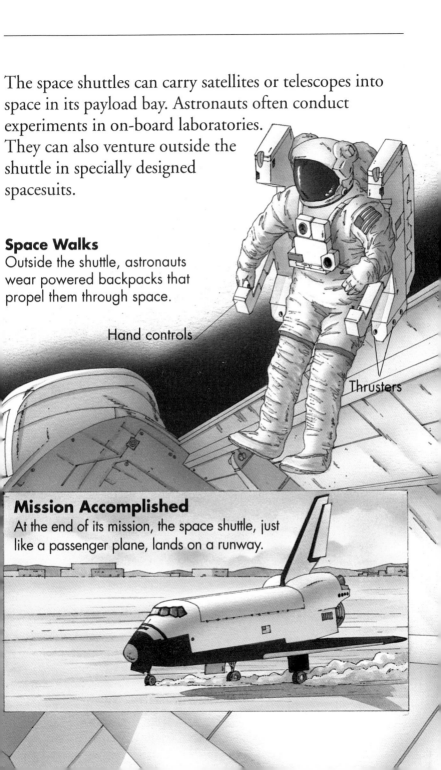

Mission Accomplished

At the end of its mission, the space shuttle, just like a passenger plane, lands on a runway.

FLYING CREATURES

Birds and insects may be nature's most famous flyers, but they are not the only animals that can fly. Some mammals and fish perform amazing feats in the air, too.

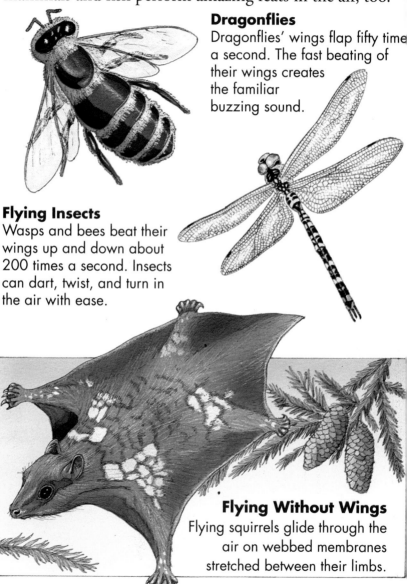

Dragonflies
Dragonflies' wings flap fifty times a second. The fast beating of their wings creates the familiar buzzing sound.

Flying Insects
Wasps and bees beat their wings up and down about 200 times a second. Insects can dart, twist, and turn in the air with ease.

Flying Without Wings
Flying squirrels glide through the air on webbed membranes stretched between their limbs.

Gliding Hawks
Like glider planes, birds such as eagles and hawks ride thermals, gliding without beating their wings.

Bat Wings
Although they are mammals, bats fly by flapping their wings as birds and insects do.

Flying Fish
Despite their name, these fish don't really fly. They build up speed while swimming, then take off from the surface and glide for a few seconds.

AMAZING FLIGHT FACTS

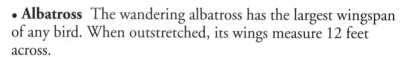

- **The Fast Falcon** The fastest flying animal is the peregrine falcon. It can fly 168 miles per hour when swooping to catch its prey.

- **Paper Plane** The longest indoor flight by a paper plane, launched by hand, is 193 feet.

- **Around the World** In 1986, two pilots flew around the world without stopping for fuel. They travelled a total of 25,000 miles in nine days in a plane called *Voyager.*

- **Albatross** The wandering albatross has the largest wingspan of any bird. When outstretched, its wings measure 12 feet across.

- **High Flyers** In 1991, two hot-air balloons, *Star Flyer I* and *Star Flyer 2,* floated over the top of Mount Everest, the world's tallest mountain.

- **Long-Distance Butterflies** Every fall, monarch butterflies migrate thousands of miles from Canada and the northern United States to Mexico. They can fly 620 miles without stopping to feed.

- **Bat Vision** Although it has very poor eyesight, a bat can fly in the dark without bumping into things. It "sees" by sending out sound waves that bounce off objects in its path.

- **Honeybee Language** By flying in circles, wagging its body, and vibrating its wings, a honeybee tells other bees how far a nectar source is from the hive.

GLOSSARY

Airfoil The special shape of a wing or propeller blade that causes air to flow faster over the top than the bottom. It helps create lift.

Biplane A plane with two sets of wings.

Drag A force that slows down an object moving through the air. Drag occurs because an object must push air out of the way as it moves.

Gondola A cabin that hangs underneath an airship. The flight deck of an airship is usually inside the gondola.

Gravity The force that pulls objects toward Earth. Gravity is what gives things weight.

Hydrogen A highly explosive gas that is lighter than air. Hydrogen was once used in airships to make them rise.

Jettison To throw out equipment or cargo to lighten a vessel.

Lift The upward force needed to overcome gravity. It keeps a bird or plane in the air. Lift is created when air flows faster over the curved upper surface of the wing than under it.

Mach number How fast a plane is going compared to the speed of sound. Mach 1 equals the speed of sound. Mach 2 is twice the speed of sound. A supersonic plane flies faster than Mach 1.

Orbiter The plane-like part of a space shuttle that carries the crew and cargo.

Payload The load carried by an air or spacecraft, such as passengers, satellites, or cargo.

Speed of sound 760 miles per hour at sea level. It varies with altitude.

Taxi To operate an aircraft on the ground before takeoff and after landing.

Terminal Main building in an airport where passengers purchase tickets, check their baggage, or find services such as restaurants and newsstands.

Thermal A rising current of warm air.

Thrust The push that keeps a plane or bird moving through the air. Thrust is needed to counter the effects of drag.

Triplane A plane with three sets of wings.

INDEX *(Entries in **bold** refer to illustrations)*